Place-Discipline *culls, cleaves, and retextures language in the service of non-totalizing modes of formal and prosodical attentions that powerfully intensify the stakes and commitments of poetry. Jose-Luis Moctezuma tends the striations, variegations, and substrata of translingual, transcultural, and transhistorical materiality. Moctezuma activates the sonic, the polymetric, and the haptic not as a palliative to the incessant, coercive logics of empire, but to potentiate futural past present temporalities that mobilize the unterritorialized in oneself, in perception itself.*

MYUNG MI KIM

Too many contemporary poets are stuck to the tones of the prefabbed social, piping up and down the scales of shared "national" definition. So it's rare and exciting to encounter a poet who deftly dials into cross-cultural microtonalities that make visible the spectral historicities of Imperium's time-&-space trickery. Jose-Luis Moctezuma aims his political scope at the psychic rootwork of our past-present moment, finding pathways out into sun-dappled new vistas and desires. The hard won futurism implicit there bespeaks of a new cartography where syncretism has become autochthony. Strange to even utter it, but Place-Discipline *is the latest mutation of the Whitman-Marti-Cesaire complex, and the democratic entanglements are still us.*

RODRIGO TOSCANO

Jose-Luis Moctezuma joins a great tradition of fabricators of America, from Melville to Pound to Charles Olson; Place-Discipline *resonates prosodically and in its knowledge-clusters with the assurance of* The Maximus Poems. *This is an establishing work. How can a Latino poet re-fabricate America and fabricate his own multiple heritages in the white world and in English? First, through a practice of dérive in the down and dirty hyperpolis. As Moctezuma's verse moves between urban zones in Chicago, a city of multiple denied, superimposed and circumscribed worlds, its rhythms shift within and against their rhythms, poised in encounter, whether stalking in reactive isolation or dancing in unison. Second, Moctezuma reverse-engineers America from the globally dispersed world city, an exploded Chicago, weaving the Hispanic and indigenous threads back in its fabric assertively. Third, he fabricates himself as an American through the cants of English from Shakespeare to Bhanu Kapil and a myriad of points between. Every page is as rich in echoes as Caliban might wish. There is wild and shocking humour in this book (I Gather the Limbs of ISIS) as well as instruction, there is rage and there is beauty. No snippets here: Pla*[   ]*through, not raided or sailed around. What an a*[   ]

JOHN WILKINSO[   ]

PLACE - DISCIPLINE

PLACE-DISCIPLINE

JOSE-LUIS MOCTEZUMA

OMNIDAWN PUBLISHING
OAKLAND, CALIFORNIA
2018

Cover art:
Dagmara Genda
detail from *Ungrounded Cities ii* (2012-2013)
ink, pencil crayon, acrylic, latex on paper
48x48in, 121.9x121.9cm
Photo courtesy of the artist

Cover and interior set in ITC Serif Gothic Std and Didot LT Std

Cover and interior design by Gillian Olivia Blythe Hamel

Offset printed in the United States
by Thomson-Shore, Dester, Michigan
On 55# Enviro Natural 100% Recycled 100% PCW
Acid Free Archival Quality FSC Certified Paper

Library of Congress Cataloging-in-Publication Data

Names: Moctezuma, Jose-Luis, 1981- author.
Title: Place-discipline / Jose-Luis Moctezuma.
Description: Oakland, California : Omnidawn Publishing, 2018.
Identifiers: LCCN 2018019994 | ISBN 9781632430595 (pbk. : alk. paper)
Classification: LCC PS3613.O29 A6 2018 | DDC 811/.6--dc23
LC record available at https://lccn.loc.gov/2018019994

Published by Omnidawn Publishing, Oakland, California
www.omnidawn.com   (510) 237-5472   (800) 792-4957
10 9 8 7 6 5 4 3 2 1
ISBN: 978-1-63243-059-5

****

"There are other worlds they have not told you of."
EL SONY'R RA, LANQUIDITY

****

"The possible is obvious. What is desired and described is the impossible.
What is not is what drives what is and transforms it into itself.
What is becomes what is not. And what is not becomes what is and what is not.
The future is always here in the past."
AMIRI BARAKA, WE TRAVEL THE SPACEWAYS

****

"In the alternate world
another alternate world."
NATHANIEL MACKEY, SONG OF THE ANDOUMBOULOU: 64

****

"The world we live in is an inclusive thing."
DAVID K. LEWIS, ON THE PLURALITY OF WORLDS

****

TABLE OF CONTENTS

Dedicated to my father,
the first poet in a "free universe"

terra em transe terra em transe terra em transe
entranced earth
limbenlaced we tremble at Zone's attrition
bodies   on the bus
read disaster crosseyed of what materializes
starry flies out   of joint
dueling realities mobbing the white-throat-
-ed cusps of reason   blank resent-
ment buttressed & steeled on Blackrock risk
management anthropo-   centric
futures harboring celestial fossil fuel fullstop
whiteness fulminant at merging   of kins
what's raised [here] is razed [there] topiaries
sculpt organisms we   are entranced by
birdsong we threnody the debt margins   we
threnody the trans-   national person-
hoods   o citizens   o myopians o timecarriers
you weren't born for yrselves   space
is apace w/ astrologies putrid from misprision
& steele glas   carcass of reciprocal
relations   race anatomies of contain-
ment   erotic derivatives bubbling
down hirsute   chests at peak oil
builders of crass   complexions
oranged where rifts   suture
Corp. seraphim to axioms   @
farthest remove from idiom   [a
foam] at end of world[s]   a foam
at the mouth of   ['the global'] law
of the excluded   [middle]   is there a
a globe to   speak of   is there a globule
sliding   down the steele glas at 4 o'clock
logo   the stars read into disjuncture astro
pro-   jective volta   what's known as
percept   management   reversal of

what gazes   back from drowned
towers hierarchies   of tomb-encased
twitter-handles   how do we know
him from   adam or statecraft non-
linear re-   gress of no use for Erra's
errata   Subartu's woes extend from
its   chronic misuse   of Tigris's live
feed   the whole world is watching
the whole   world on wireless auto-
erotic suicide   gash in the wires
gorge down your   spine   pineal
gland asphyxiated   foam at
eyelids of rivers   pipelines un-
seen as petrol   is in rock   chulla-
chaqui un-   weaves the molar of its
skinsack   where the rain seeps in &
mold   gathers   it conjures precarity
in   the glacial crevices heedless of 5th
sun   a book of faces to store our affects   &
dis-   affections   let's see their faces let's see
'em   emerge unwashed from pools of screen
the head on video   drome shorn of its torso
infrared scopes are set upon us   a feeding
of the 7000000000   they are already
choking on brine   the salmon have somehow
learned to speak spanish   & they curse us
the shareholders & rapturists   are rejoicing
they cremate their cares   they tunnelize on
the tube   where's your ghost at   white owl
or blackjack   if you're in doubt   juke it
        burn it all make your feet work
stand on the rock we swarm blkrock we stand
        limbenlaced   earthentranced
in the desert place   where white dwarfs eat us
        & the caiman soothes our name

:: came to chicago, undernourished &
    winded as it were, unsensing
of the spatialization of river-speak
    because Meridian, because
nel mezzo del cammin di nostra vita
    overplays its aged incantatory
burdens on the mediocrities of mid-
    way contraband & the flatnesses
overcome by spotted skylark. Here-
    tofore the particulars of
local pride suggested in lakeshore
    leisure-cruise by road, in
disguising what oppositions attract
    or dissemble :: came here &
did not partition, yet partitions
    manifest, divisions & diversities
of some neglected racial nature still
    inquisitive of mythic wrath
or, anyway, gentried into subsets
    of blanched privilege :: fire came
& did not come, the absent froth of
    tensionless lake water, hard
put to it, this patterning that does
    not invite but segregates,
sunders but does not ask history inside
    for a drink only looks away —
does not color in the books but stores winter
    as uniform, the collateral
face of homeless and fear-debauched
    citizenry, in a capital of
secondary fulminations :: checagou
    skunkz & damnation ::

****

:: blueblack delineament of a megapolis
        panopticized by police
and what renders identity
the false habituation of color—
      —line   redlineblue—
       —linegreenlineorange—
—linepurplelinebrownline

                  the L
           of songlines
                 ritualized
          & uncrossed

    an elevation
    impossibilitated
    by flatland —

                    — a dreaming systematized
           by bacterial auto— suggestion
                to lay down these arms   to
         lie supine and   assume the scale
              of the land's indirections

    el lago un espejo
    de virtudes ::
    :: the lake a lay
    of homologies

＇

****

****

        :: think of this crystal
        gemmed at lakeedge
        think of this
        centrifuge

                rainbowed &
                radiating landward

inviting otherness
to sleep subwise
& reduce our midway
recalcitrance to whiteness

        think of brazil, of a future cosmic
            imaginary ::
        think of nuclear fusion
      think of ghostnotes   ((in the drum
        but don't think
        of its depth
          as theology   ((the pulsing We
                    of our Us
          no all but in us

:: *uma cidade*
em preto e azul ::

****

17

MEGAPOLISOMANCY

```
****
*****
******
*******
********
*********
**********
```

At any particular time of history there have always been one or two cities of
the monstrous sort—viz., Babel or Babylon, Ur-Lhassa, Nineveh, Syracuse,
Rome, Samarkand, Tenochtitlan, Peking—but we live in the Megapolitan (or
Necropolitan) Age, when such disastrous blights are manifold and threaten to
conjoin and enshroud the world with funebral yet multipotent city-stuff. We need
a Black Pythagoras to spy out the evil lay of our monstrous cities and their foul
shrieking songs, even as the White Pythagoras spied out the lay of the heavenly
spheres and their crystalline symphonies, two and a half millennia ago.

FRITZ LEIBER, *Our Lady of Darkness*, 64

```
**********
*********
********
*******
******
*****
****
```

****

at the city gates ::
plutocrats of the highest potentate
positioned a plaque

on which shone
4 étoiles sur
Nouvelle France

riven in coruscations
that scald the skin at six points
in pale fevered light

:: and through me
the gnashing of teeth
nella città dolente

****

****

on their expeditions
they assembled
moral genealogies of a trifling
nature ::

that
Tartary obscured
a 4th Hank
to upstage the others

that
Quebec emerged
unscathed from Champlain's venous hands
in 1608 ::

maybe Kanada keeps passageways into Spice Roads,
the indianless Indies

& maybe Champlain pictured Lake Huron
in 1617

but
what do we know
of Jesuit cunning among the Hurons ::

only scarcity & meat

****

****

//
scientia est potentia
a city webbed in its warfares & state
    craft, art of inter-
        jections
                she walks on the western untoward

      ((& degrees of freedom shall release you

lines scatter the splendid reversals

      & degrees of freedom shall release you((

the We of our supremacy   whiteness un-
                principled in the "imagination(s)
      we know of"
           a field calls us
    precedes
    our knowing, hearkened
    by color, spectrum (@) rose
    \\

****

****

of the word's eyewound (@)

                     we know little

of what they know

             who speak in the *lengua*

     of spectrum

     a new wire —   —less paradigm

        imagination(s)

        senza fili   somewhere in

                   Hartford

     the lines christ—

   —cross &

         lure the static conversations

              & blank men

              busy at conversion

        encode the stagnant crystals

****

****

the increasingly crowded clouded electromagnetic spectrum spools
    in which we traffic our personae on interstellar
        spaceways ((no, not the future ((
           pastness past
                what ratchets kin's concomitants
                to foreign cormorants
                    perched
                on death's arborescence ((
           swoops
& regresses timecults, transforms wing
into scale, slows living systems down
sprouts serpent-feather, turns
tardigrade
        bcuz
           the Dharma
of DARPA
        "redounds in being"
as above, so below—
           abbreviations in a virtual C++
domained in
           finite awareness
animal futures
           ((becomings, goings
an orientation of
almost objects

        what they designate
        "the new flesh"

****

****

[O.O.O.] heed yr locksmiths
mind da gaps in yr A E S T H E T I C S
anthropocentric   미 래 가
blues on vape
recyclable futures last F O R E V E R
of what T.I.A. in I.R.L.   없 다
time-reverses &
signals

        in fresh & outworn
        dictations // *dictée* of the
        "Autonomous.
           Self-generating."
       Floral shoppes.
    vectoral dividends
a politics of the *thing*
thinged
object lessons
in how terrorists are entrained
into total subjects©
deoxygenated prisoners of T.M.I.
deep in the tranches
as they turn fish   as their wounds scale upward
their mouths in swamp

****

****

zoöpraxiscope
& zapruder in the fun   house
mass violences in private   phantasy
walls behind walls behind   walls   in the court-
houses   on the grassy knolls   on 18th Street
interpellate
the ism of situation
as to where
terrorists manifest parasitic flows
what you call   *difference engine*
what they call   *geopolitics*   nodes
detourned from a cast net vibrato
expert
witnesses
of syncopes & d' quincey's
choice oscillations ::

(the) future   forever :: serial   black   ))beach be-
          lasts   ))box   cube   neath
rhapsodic))
          pavement))non-   place   non-   lieu
(what)
          you   knew   you   *knew*

****

****

:: ntropy in lawrenceville usa
erebus in rochester usa
zylinium in gaithersburg usa
agent orange in syracuse usa
love & rockets in los angeleez usa
the cloud chamber in alexandria(n) [mythos]
         becoming-tense of cloud corp
radio cloud oneohone //

                    ntelligent radi os that care not what n-
                    telligence is   to be gained from e-raze-
                    sure wh o give s a fu ck wha tdrump f can t-
                    ruck tha t too t he spec trum speaks

:: ntelligent radi os need yr help please
go anachronic or analogic or anamorphic
or what you will, go human if you must
bury skulls or spirals in the graveyard
of yr clowns //

****

****

if you must remind yrself of yrself ((or what
sates human taste)) when they jabberwocky
on wireless)) with tremendous frequency
((bordered by scarcity *if you will we must*

we shall make you scarce friend
we shall

:: precarity in the cage of ageless mechanism
the flesh rubrics contaminate vernacular forms //
typologies of skintones for better policing

we resist this scarcity of spectrum
the spectrum pool which speaks for you speaks
to me for you   speaks of precarity speaks
of scarcity on the lower frequencies
((i speak for you
scarce of spectrum
the grid remembers you
at 3:13am w/ the lights off
as you scratch off the scabs of 24/7 disease

****

```
*********
********
*******
******
*****
****
```

                                              Lake Superior

                          like Saturn

                                              approaches orbit,

            is limned

                                              along its coast

                          in polyandrous moon-

                                    light

                                              ((Louis XIV
                              ascends in sculpted polymers
                                      1661 ::

```
****
```

****

:: the trade of crude men

at odds w/

what corridors

in the dark render up

::

cracks

of blueblack

wilderness

in skeletal

outline

river otters

who taper &

cry out

profligate

cadences

sing the

distances

to sleep ::

****

```
*********
*********
********
*******
******
*****
****
```

of bldgs changed to various forms i sing
celestial descent of city crust
the mountaining that savage men call hi-
rise   metrical fractures in lengthening
of time's inefficient refuse   the scene-
ography dotted in microchip skulls
nature's face transfigured, if we can call
it a face   :: corroded   internecine   ::
disease   deprivation   disorder   death
stacked horrendous one upon the other
& above :: absence of struggle   presence
of difference's non-presence   views from 6
corners of hexagrammic precision
reduction of space for lower caste cells
elevation of access for labor's
abstractionists   ::   incorporated en-
tities   vacant penthouses   disorganed
bodies   sons of sons of sheiks   men of gold

entire blocks in moneyed solitude   ::
kultur in some vague decomposition
the hip as lure for cool consumerist
individuation   appropriative
of 'ethnic' 'ethnicity'   otherness
absorbed into greater apparatus
repurposing of bldgs repurposed
in whiteness   false consciousness of blank page
trades black syntax as if it were substrate
as if it were monolith   amongst
homo laborans   a geomancy
to bind all others   to decapitate
black (inner) thought   to desacralize [black
lives]   in the threshing fields   homo sacer
what can be butchered   w/ impunity
amongst the color-eyed police   open-
carry proof for open-parry   prisons
of the mind in symmetry w/ dragnets

****
*****
******
****
****
****
****

****

of those creviced

in their
        scrawled

insurgencies

        ****

        scattered as leaves

   & pluralized

        in the waste

of "neither sun

      nor death"

****

****

their white magick is such:

what is raised   [here]
          is razed   [there]
what is relayed   [here]
          is delayed   [there]

****

     of ether

         moon-

light or

          erasure

****

****

the circean foam we've become:

an apolitics
　　　　　of rootless

communal
　　　　forms

　　　　　　　　like cattle & hogs

　　snorting in zero-sums

　　　　　　　lycanthropy
as respite

　　　　from being human
　　　　　　　　　　& a likening

　　　　　　　of the Event
　　　to simulacrum
　　　　　　　　　　　or its return,
　　　　　　　　　　　　　　again

　　　　in the Book
　　　　　　　　of Faces

****

****

foot-
      less activisms, be-
hooved
          tremored in their in-
dividuations
        she + he who are
   // *They*

the cyborgian // *We*

      the unpersoned *they* of our *us*
genus
            automata mille-
   ennial
     androids
the them
         // of *You*
  we,
    who are

****

****
****
****
****
******
*****
****

1663 :: Kanada regaled
but still
provincial

Outraged Iroquois
in each un-
concealed place
morphemically savaged

1665 :: Fr. Allouez
@ Chequamegon Bay

Huron & Ottawa
evacuated
or ideologued to death

****

****

Mississippi marks
where call signs are broad-
cast in the blank world   & where
Ojibwe broad-
bands its radial languages
on Channel Jiibay

lengthy as petals are
in river-
hair

((meanwhile :: Jacques Marquette
absorbs
Chequamegon   :: collapses
heavy
w/ predilections

****

****

o citizens o neo-marxians o time-capitalists
you weren't born merely for yrselves:
this country claims a fraction of yr realism
give up yr acculturations to the machine
cut off yr soft unworn hands on the steele glas
what you see in reflection predates you
   in sine waves in test patterns ((or what have you
what you unsee elects yr affinities & prezidentz

       cuz

chullachaqui sees you
  chullachaqui breathes you
chullachaqui carves open yr synapses
& gorges on what's residued
   :: that which comes at night
& absorbs the dayward
   what at 3am takes yr place
sits in yr leather plush
  & codes apocalyptic scripture
in the Book of Faces

****

```
*********
********
*******
******
*****
****
***
```

after surviving the discontents of a meadow
unsewn by winter's sterile
logic

which
in Beijing and in Papua New Guinea
and in Johannesburg

had yet been unheard of

the jesuit &
the harpsichordist
(((who spoke aboriginal
in a cleft tongue

wondered at it all ::
their gazes
swept along shadows

tracing a riverrun of broken
margins

```
***
```

****

and
they asked of the Illini

:: had it been a sacred
ghost
what lay claim to this immense yet missed
ozhigwan
in the orphic under-
growth

even
amid its scaled tributaries?

the Illini
responded
:: no,
you were only too occupied

chewing on the remains of anura

to notice its ancestry
in the particles of yr gums

****

****

if you buy out or sabotage or insure
& penury or mass-murder
or death-sicken or experiment viruses on
or stealthkill [Osage] or fuck [them]
or let rot in the streets or sweet-talk
or con or carry or stifle or injure
or divide & add-up or conquer & enslave
yr competitors

     they'll name streets & bldgs after you
     they'll suck the marrow out yr
     bone they'll suck the milk out yr
     kindness they'll placard yr
     name
       in the streets where a plague
    of faceless interlopers plead for yr coinage
      & you dream the dream
    of network marketers & say nothing
       & pass forth into frozen altars

****

****

Hubbard who massacred [   ]
[   ] Kinzie who slept w/ [   ]
LaSalle who odysseyed [   ]

                    great [   ] men
if you build nothing
if you invest in the zero-sums
if you get yrself inside the out-
        side of the inside of the stockyards
    ))the front of the yards &
        not the backside of sweetback's song
   in blue sunlight
they'll raise towers to you
& raze blackhands & letter you
broad & flaming across rivers
            & steele glas

****

```
*********
********
*******
******
*****
****
****
```

fauna
who were human
before humans were humans

this is
what is called

place-
discipline

what is called

hearing the bloodsack leap in the space
between skingaps

what is called

walking on the western untoward

```
****
```

****

what is known as

the color in the volcano's
eyewound

what resists

the lettering on our backs of the symbols of illiteracy

what breathes

at night in defiance of
the artifice
of white immune systems

what is called gnosis *the walking of one place*
to the next place

what is called
The Dreaming

****

****

((a brief history
         of tiny (invisible) hands in the dark((

****

****

taxonomy ::
　　of bacteria of
:: globule capital

citicorp decomposes
into citigroup ((a traveler's group

　　　　　　　　or the highwaymen, the quarry
　　　　　　discharged
　　/ euro-ameri-bank /　　　　banamex((
　　　　　　　　chase mannahata for 60 guilders
　　　　((what a deal
coins jp
　　　　morgan chase ((wash our

mutual interests / great west-　　　ern finance // ah!

　　　　　　　　　　　　　manson family /
　　dimes bancorp / first　　chicago / banc　　1 / 1st
　　　　　　commerce /
　　　　　　　　jpmorgan le fay / on relay
chemtrails
　　　　　　-lyric bank / bear the stern ursa major
　　　　& ursa sub-
　　　　　　prime))
　　america's　　　　　　　　bank
　　　　　　　　[because
　　　l'amerika lycans
　　　　　　　　homo homini
　　　　　　　　　lupus est

****

46

****

in-
existent ex-
cept in name & ab-
stention] :: (("U.S."
trust [us] / m[ega] b[ucks] n[ary] a /
con-   tinental bank / bank-
on america / security pacific *ban*
corps /   nations bank / fleet
financial group / bancboston holdings / bay
banks / summit *ban*   *lieue* / ujb
financial / country
wide financial /
merrill   lynch)) well
's fargo re-
mainder ((human song   well   's farrago
[defies in-   corp-   oration
monikers
survive   segregation]
((1st inter-
state *ban*   *corps* /
nor   west hold   ingco. /
south
trust / w(h)ack
ovia / central fidelio / co   restate / deepstate
fingering / 1st   union /
the
[eternal] moneystore))

****

****

El Hombre en la Torre Oscura

*"Snipers were a problem for many years. These people would set up in a window
of the towers and just shoot at anyone. Two police got killed. I remember one day,
a cop car was sent to my building and someone was sniping at them from the
building facing my lot. And one young girl I remember seeing, she had on a trench
coat. She was really running across the lot. When she got to the building, the back
of her coat had caught a whole lot of buckshot. It was a miracle she wasn't hurt."*

Dolores Wilson, former resident of the Chicago Housing Authority's
Cabrini-Green public housing development, in conversation with
Audrey Petty, *High Rise Stories: Voices from Chicago Public Housing*

*"Every school in America needs to immediately identify, dedicate and deploy
the resources necessary to put these security forces in place right now. And the
National Rifle Association, as America's preeminent trainer of law enforcement
and security personnel for the past 50 years, is ready, willing and uniquely
qualified to help."*

Wayne LaPierre, Executive Vice-President of the NRA, Dec. 21, 2012

****

****

                       from a great height in CGI

                         a "lone wolf" automaton

               in a torn sweat-soaked tank-top

peers out   from the window blind

                            & adjudicates

                       the profit margins

from the 36th chamber   he locks &

         loads a .220 Swift caliber rifle

                    the click is clean

            the high sun burns the glass

                 a web of sweat beads

                       his forehead

            the miserly fan wheezes

              in the thickset room

& he sucks in   heavy encrusted air

                a transfigured sigh

             of various incantations

           he sees holes in the fore-

          heads of two of the undead

            strolling the parking lot

              "shots were fired"

from a high-rise   the incantations commence

           a 57-year-old man's throat

          splits open while conversing

w/ brethren post church organ's reprieve

             outside the temple

           the men in the high tower

remain unknown

****

****

they see holes
in the black foreheads white fore-
heads of unknown reptiles
whose motives outside the scales
of human compassion
are obscure
for whom freedom extends no further
than warm texture   of wood-carved action
he shoots w/ extremest
prejudice   or what they called
"race" in those days
the sweating man on the 36th
reads in Blackrock scrolls the runes
of shrewdest gamble
"risk management"   or what baptizes the fore-
heads what fills them up   the holes
in the rostrums of whitefaced men   who
dress, & fall, & utter   the assorted samenesses   he
tolerates the pores in his own face   a void
of disintegrate flesh
severed by blackhole time-
schedules there are punctures
in the sound-fabric of his apartment &
"culture"   cannot answer for them
when he reaches for the arsenals
of declination //

****

50

****

                                                & what thru
                         "lack of motive"
serves as motive: *a climate of hunter*
                       like heat patterns in
            spectral nightvision, the rage
       that sets the windup dolls to fulminate
     at the concupiscent blur of organism
                          & colorlines
    the automaton clocks in
     hearing everything   it gleans consecrated
whispers   of an old woman on the phone
                        w/ her son in Mobile
      it   hears
                   violation of unseen
         bodies tense animalized   it
                  senses the crack
             that barcodes these bodies
                     into networks
              of recidivist contagion
   it   stands a-
          part from its bandwidth it
     "aims true" at their assemblage   it
disrupts   the chords of their gathered voice   it
                    hears immense
   breathing heavy slow   murmurs
               of a 10-year-old girl
                    suffocating
                  on glass shards
              a bullet coughing
                 in her throat

****

****

<pre>
                                   the clocks won't quit their
          running   the dogs are quiet
                                         it senses
                                           that
                                     day has for night
       traded places   and
                                         the wicks
                                   are ground down
                                      to stumps
                                           it
                                         hears
                                        stereos
   gathering fractured silence   erasing
                                   noise of what stays
                                     news out-
                                   side the broken towers
                                        out-
                                   side the "antiphonal
                                      carillons" &
                                   their rubbed out faces
of "the autumnal, the wounded"   projects on the
                                          plain
</pre>

****

****

he tweets:

control them from the out-
side of the out-
side
          where they can only gaze up &
cast
impotent figs at heaven

          permit them to be
scandalized,
                    self-righteous

****

mega-
polis-
omancy:

rendre la puissance publique
impuissante

****

****

Robert Taylor Homes

in the shadow of zero-sums
towers rise

the alabaman architect
mocked by racial
projects
bearing his
insignia

falls over & coughs

ponders ::

what is visibility

:: this
delusion

that rises

cramped &
stunted

as sunflower
in white palisades
of megapolis

****

****

Chicago School

they call it 'human

kapital'
the closing of the gates
closing
of the schools   closing
of the
vertical))   ((mindscapes
a prairie
through which
energy passes
'convulsive'
as beauty is
under-
neath the   pulse of horizon-
talized relations
the global only
a decimal point away
in Oak Park   in Santiago
de Chile
in Jakarta
not gargantuan
governance, nor gangsterism

****

rather ::
   small & infinite
      fractures
where ::
   the musk wind seeps in

   where ::
      they won't know
what ails them
        ((the scent of skunz
   or onion tears
       phantom position-
ings
   of non lieu,
      source-
less

    :: checagou
     uber alles

****

```
*********
********
*******
******
*****
****
****
```

                                   communication
    effected
    by water

    Great Lakes – Illinois – Gulf of Mexico

    a missing channel
    on the tube

    its elemental architecture,
    a media convoluted by
    convergence

    & fuckeries
    of a gnostic nature

```
****
```

****

what is called fake
news

:: is what stays news
in
the luminous increate

dark, trumpeted

by
infidels

****

****

CTA

in be-
tween the acts
the sud-
den violence
inter-
weaves
the world-
ing of cig-
arette barters
& burnt discs
"packs packs
packs"
he says
when the door opens
& the sleeper
awakes

another world
larger than this
inter-
stice inter-
rupts our
ordinances

****

****

"you can have
one loosie
or two,
20/20 eyesight
is one-
pack

:: is *contra mundum*
what rules the rules
around me"

:: an art of the hidden

vices of a less habitual nature ::
chance operations
enmeshed & quartered in the vicinity
of lakeedge &
speedrail

cigarette burn emblematic
of crude waltzes
in dub housing

the gentry fly by in streamers
expatiated
unremarked
their manner of annotating the spaces
in between
zonal lure
& bldg crevice

****

****

"i know of lofts structures edifices
heightenings
that push back on you
& swarm yr insides

as a virus loose on the eyelids

"i know of what converses
with the whistling
prairie air

gone astray from broad acreage

& inexplicable

disappeared
as fires are, their causations

in Taliesin

****
*****
******
****
****
****
****

I GATHER THE LIMBS OF ISIS

a binary to bind all others in their iniquity ::
    ISIS recruits [the arm of Mohammed], [the swollen feet of Christ]
        the circularity that is called
        paideuma
                a living fire innarded
        by islamic statehoods
        piecemealed &
            quartered
            given the loving & lonesome &
                lissome fingers of ISIS
  death from above

                    she writes letters
                    to syrian daughters
              asking them
          to support the
      troops
              death is no organism
                  in the radio
                      silence

     Set the clocks on their wash
         cycles :: bodies of boys in their atomic
            simplicity :: Osiris in their shadow-struck pupils

drone from above

ISIS pieces together Osiris
from remnants of corporate person-
hoods, her jeweled
grievances on Horus's
lap, the ankh
framing falcon-
headed distances
in nomenclature
of bird sex ::

(the) islamic state of
iraq &
syria
( ) islamic state
of iraq
& the levant
or

( ) pharmaceutical company
based in Carlsbad, CA
manufacturer of
"antisense, a technology
that aims to treat disease at the genetic level
using oligonucleotides,"

ISIS gathers
           "the [lego] blocks of DNA"
       and tetrises together
                   "libraries of molecules"

she allies herself
       with pharma-
               giant
((Boehringer Ingelheim
       International G.m.b.H.
               "of Germany"
                       for the sake of goddess reach
across seas

       the limbs of Osiris
               are numberless
       as the first-
quarter stocks
       in after-
               noon daylight,
                       as dust in levantine
               wand, her caduceus
                       fuses the snake
       to its tongue

       DAESH
       DAISH
       ((death)

               DAESH
               DAISH
               ((death)

DAESH
DAISH
(death))

DAESH
DAISH
(death))

in rojava
she walks on the western untoward

          mastering limbs
in Ma'at's photo-negatives ::

    "i have not mastered virtuosity
     i have not mastered spectacle
     i have not mastered the two tongues of the pale snake
     i have not mastered the waters or the winedark seas
          or my own heart
     i have not mastered mastery

     i have not

She left home, she set out for the world. For the world was a vast museum. In her
Eyes, he was all eyes, when he saw the archaic smile, the approach of a nonbinary
travels, even by the first residence abroad, she swiftly learned that the chief end
freeing him to receive his own image in the omphalos, two eagles do not make one
of modern cities, of those townships that had graduated from interminable wars
he thought, leaving the circle of his relations does not set one free, he is a they anyway,
and the clash of cell-spliced relativities, which were nourished by the ideological
transmissions of other earths drove him away from an island of genders and from
capital of historical progressiveness, was to resemble museums in their liturgical
those that in their familiarity with him believed they knew exactly what was
isolation, in their redoubtable commerce, in their intentional design,
best for his body, and yet knew him not to the depths. So had he thought. He left
in the open-form to exegetical generation. Architecture produced its own
because his own home had not circumference; he daily contemplated the
climates, since the natural world, the old vegetable world, had been disposed of
fantasy of leaving the Father's House, that he may rupture the herculean mansplainers
spectacularly, with terrific burials under pavement and statues and bureaucracies.
and find what worth he had in a sea of male indifference, or what corrosive inertia,
The obtuse gentrification of the suburbs that were formerly disreputable districts,
what finite infinitudes, what the nature in nature's nature was inside, without
which had been reputable mansions before they fell out of reputation, into the
the nescience of affection attached to the sensation of knowing; could these
fashionable micro-chateaux known as warehouses and loft-spaces, once more as
concepts exist outside of his apprehensions in a material way, in an ancient city
if in a nutshell of the lux aeterna, even if they were silently invaded later by a
whose avenues are inexplicably made known to him outside of any possible
clandestine flux of communities that irrigated their clan origins beneath nonsites
foreknowledge, or whether an appointment kept on the bridge of lovers could
of wealth, in countless parodies of mothertongue, who spoke in lexemes that
have the same resonance in his heart as it had when he read the tragic history of
had not to the astonishment of the empire-builders been soaked up by the
a few hastened polar nights? Like a famed object of art beheaded of its Capital, he
business-speak sponge, but who were anyhow inhospitably driven out by the

dreamt of encountering the crepuscular soul of a city that would overwhelm the

creative-capitalist secret weapon known as the re-gentrification of open boxes,

paltry toys of memory which so frequently cloud the clever apprentice's sightlines.

would flower in insomnia, would suffer 24/7 disease, would spill forth in a

Yes, maybe the architecture of a city would silently judge him, he, preceded by

surplus of streets and signs and zero-sums perpetually built and rebuilt

billions who had flown in everyday on redeyes, long before they ever dreamt it up,

and heaped on top of open-closed boxes, department stores, and cinema

he who was no better than they, indeed, they, the poets-in-transit who had raised

multiplexes. A perpetual emptiness was the rule of the game, a game for barons

the renown of the grandiose cities they visited, who far surpassed all that he

and destructionists, to vacate every possible ecosystem and make complete the

had achieved, all that he could possibly imagine achieving; they had written

organism by removing the organs. It came to a point that a city had not to be

books, odes, elegies, marvelous compositions on the secret life of cities; they

inhabited, to be a city. A chessboard robbed of its pawns, an empty page filled

had razed a city in a night of manias and raised it again in three days with a

with, erased, re-filled by, deprived of, convergent-divergent lines, and squares

single line, a phrase, a word that would upon its utterance enchant the air

and staircases, and shallow ends marked by deep gulfs, and high windows leading

and immediately bring into its compass the buildings, the people, the sounds,

to miniature ceilings, and plastic park paths unpeopled, and blown up by the

the whole city brought to life to one's monstrous astonishment. What could he

sudden appearance of canals and the continuous riot of construction. The city no

do, when all he'd written were minor notes on the lives of ordinary people, in the

longer had to be a structure imposing its own laws, it had to be a navigation, a

space of a windowless room at night while his custom-saturated family slept in

reiteration, a conduction of transparent currents, a ritual negotiation, a steerage

the air-conditioned room, unaware of the disproportion between what he

to the astro-inertial, toward the cyber-tectonic, the inassimilable, the inaccessible

envisioned when he inhabited maps and paintings, and poems devoted to the

domain of the inward. Museums are constantly being reupholstered, or they

remembrance of supreme towns and immortal metropolises, and the feeble dusty

perish. Cities are constantly being bombarded by chains and outlets, or they pass

room he shared with his sisters? It was not that he wished to prove to himself

away. Yes, she learned that commerce (commerce!), the backbone of the city, the

that he wore someone else's body or that someone else was inside him, an Other who

bloodline, would transmogrify, would lactate, would swell, would atrophy; an

held his hand in that moment-monumentalizing 'sacred rage' which brought people
exhibit of fallacies, one day the price of gold, the next on red-tag sale, truth
and androids to recognize the angelic disposition in themselves, their transitive
turned cheap in a domain of amores pasajeros. Who now are the true and more
metamorphism & interstitial oneness in the embrace of other transcendental identities;
enthused residents of a city? Tourists no doubt. And she was among them. The
no, he set out into the world because the world had ceased to exist for him;
time of alchemists was long past, a relic of the old patrimony, a deceased
because the cartographers had scoured all that was to be known and could be
celebration of inordinate dependencies, of euclidean sex and concealed
known about the world, each region of the earth marked, each island situated,
monies; she was rather invigorated with abstract impulses that counseled her in
each city on the island dotted with flags; because his home was deprived of
private whenever she met with opposition or with the predictable resentment of
history, since it had already achieved what civilization had promised and what
those on the other side of the river, those of the opposite persuasion who thought
culture had surmised; because the sun was hot, and in his room he sweated and
themselves worthy of unreasonably biased dispute. She was no more a woman
heard a whirr at the backs of the classrooms that were outside his window in
than a man could be; but men persisted being toxins. The city was alive with tasks
the nearby school, and he knew he had grown too old when he heard the chatter
and opportunities that pointed toward motile and renewable leisure-zones. She
of children rebounding from the ball courts, and the voices of exuberance meting out
did not have to possess an 'identity' or an ostensive praxis or a laminated calling
each boundary in the circumvented public school, glad as they were to have
card. She knew that post-op practices resumed any such ipseities which fulfilled
no thoughts of their own save those of hopscotch, homework, and sleep. Yes,
the drivel of patriarchal codeswitches that would impress the gate-keepers and
he went abroad because there was absolutely nothing he could do at home that
blind the middle-managers, if they had not already succumbed to a species of
would attract the world's attention and bring it to the doorstep of a small town
envy that was predominantly self-aggrandizing. She could, from her island of
adrift in the inland empire, yet unknowing that it was unseen in the desert, and stuck
independence in a citadel run amok with walls so large they were skies and with
perennially, vilely, in between shopping districts, strip malls, and massive parking
liberties so vaguely and freely drawn that they were multiple, with hoarders,
lots; because he had no choice, there was nothing vital or honest that could
reactionaries, predators, financiers, insurance agents, and the old guards who

force him to improve himself or better the predictable and the worst in him;

preserved a system incapable of housing her self-realized customs – she could,

because in the stagnation of his room framed by paperbacks and compact discs

for she had the power to, deny the wolves their meat-eating. She would not

and the brutal desk and the iron-frame chair, and the heavy and slow computer,

sacrifice the smallest part of her volition for a guarantee of favor in the luxuriant

there grew in him the outrageous seed of lust that gnawed in his vacant heart,

neighborhoods. She thought this, that "freedoms" would be freed from their

in his mild hands, and in the sawdust ends of his bare feet; and because he

intransigent myth, once she had shown that their egress proceeded from an

had no means of enjoying walks without hearing the obnoxious roar of traffic,

enslavement to the anachronic idea that identity was a fixed state, when in

where everywhere patrolled and flashed and honked and hovered that awful

practice and in point of truth it was an insuperable intervention, a mechanism of the

inhuman mechanistic concatenation of cars; and because he had nowhere

highest order available to *homo laborans*, which still deserved her full attention and

to walk to, and he had very little to aspire becoming; because the world had

implementation; these thoughts were hers when she visited the Centre Pompidou

quickly run itself tired, had obliterated all trace of the heroes of classical virtue,

& the Guimet in Paris, or the Abattoirs in Toulouse; when she walked through the

and had manufactured in place the simplistic easily reproducible beauties that,

exposed spinal cord of the City of Arts & Sciences in Valencia, or through the

far from demanding more work-spirit or refinement of focus, instead relied on

narrow gutted hull of the Kiasma in Helsinki. And in a promenade through the

the speed of their appearance, on a pure, incontestable, high-definition retinal display

gates of Babylon at the Pergamon, she pondered the validity of archaeology, for

that would streamline any marketplace in the world order and come away

seeing that it came to this, the transport of an entire and strictly unknown

unscathed by the competing innovations of others; beauties that were a single

civilization to an artificial island in Berlin, what was real anymore? What was

product, a modus operandi, that could not possibly absorb 'essences' or severed

history in the face of innovation and technology? Nothing could be preserved

ontologies of ennatured causes, but would be as impenetrable as the unrecyclable

really, and frankly it was all made up – a blank slate erased and copied and re-

plastics buried deep in the earth that will not be broken down in a hundred

erased and re-copied; it did not matter if in a courtyard between the two wings of

four-score years unless the earth consume and unburden itself; inorganic beauties

the Uffizi at Firenze, she had a vision of the summation of beauty, that beauty

that will, rather than fabricate wars or flourish in peace-time, mystify the spheres
was, indeed, a mortal voluptuous lust, an exquisite zombie walking blindly
and lull them with white noise, into a comatose waste land tremored by gross
through a marble blue-checkered hallway; or that at the Reina Sofia in Madrid
indigestion, by the inability of the organs to break down the polyethylene corpses
she witnessed a synchrony of cities in a luminous window by Delaunay, that in
they have been force-fed and which they cannot expel without damaging the integrity
fact she could delineate from that one vantage point, housed in the contemporary
of a constitution that affirms that corporations are people too. The abysmal
gallery that had once been a hospital wing reserved for dying soldiers, the
futureless future oppressed him, this so-called 'futurity' that promised no end,
simultaneous appearance of the founding of Rome 700 years BC and the
and thus was full of The End, heading not in one linear direction, but in every
founding of Dubai in 1971, the former bathed in a contrast of moon-shadow and
direction simultaneously, remorselessly, without the least regard for limitation,
pastorals, the latter blasted in a garish crimson sunlight. To glimpse invisible
nor a minute conception of the natural imperfection that guides the living and
cities pattern will suffice – the pattern is one of time. In the Vitra Design
the dead to make a place on the autonomous earth and learn from its rotations
Museum she had a daydream of a tranquil home-life, her eyes drowsy from
and its gaian resistances. In the cities of the dead there is no end in sight, one
gazing on passive beckoning chairs and tables floating unperturbed in space, but
can't get by without a map, or a metro station, or a taxi, or a sidewalk, or an Uber,
she quickly dissolved the idea – she had no 'home' but the World, and the world
or a bus, or a partner to talk with, or a lover to bed, or a bar to drink at, or a
was an immeasurable continuous museum, an inorganic world, a world that
friend to house for a week, or a magazine to read, or a book to look up, or a
appeared static but which was vibrating insanely within its distance-gorged
website to check, or an institution to apply to, or an internship to seek, or a
interior – and with these thoughts in her mind, as she descended the spiral
blog to update for the international exchange. And with these thoughts in
staircase from heaven in the Vatican Museum, the orphic mirror caught her, &
mind, the prodigal wanderer rose up from his iron-frame chair, and turned off
she laid eyes on him, rising up to paradise, who also laid eyes on her, knowingly.
the heavy humming PC, knowingly. He would leave home; he would set out for the world.

blackhawk
as
logos /// \\\
     in the beginning
were
     the We
((scipio
moorhead's rage   @
visibility

                 ((or wheatley's "solemn gloom of night"
                  that shuts the doors of sight

     what is
     visibility
         of the colored dead

         in Essanay?

((no better indio than
         a [ ] one
   [hahaha]

why do you see—
immediate as you are— what you see
in— sine waves   ((pincushion
     mandalas
        what
this vacuum tube
        ((in hertz
distorts
     [ ]

why is absence
or the sum of land
disputes
staked on a chill spectacle

                of bodies armored & bladed

      at pretend-war

                        [   ]

                      why is

the afterlife of logos
resonant & fecund

            of what absence draws
                in blacksand

     [   ]

         why is
the red one crossing mississippi again

((these borders aren't zoned
for crossing
        you know)
               why is blackhawk at the whites
again
        why are indians called indians
when they play baseball

who were they when
they weren't ballin'

or stitched on cotton fabric

                                        ((manufactured in thailand
in indonesia   in sri lanka

                                        ((who were the indians
in bangalore

                    stitching in neat lines
                    these grinning beheaded red faces

what was cleveland when the browns were there
                    when cuyahoga shed flammable shieldskin

& senecas spilt
oshinika
at choice removal
                                        in monoscope

in bad axe :: spafford
the killing of 4 white men

      is massacre

but systems removal rape starvation scalping disinheritance forced marriage
                    of *indígenas* ::

      is jurisprudence

[hahaha]

      the sauks knew wolves were changed into men
      black hawk knew he was to be ingested
      or suffer the quill pen's penal colony tattooage
      they reserved for them a place
      in NW where the fruits
      tasted of seasalt and the hares spoke koans

what is this life as a logo
              [ ]
                    reserved to be on the apparel
of lucre outfits
& men of minor athletic carapace

even bearded men kanadians russians
lithuanians
      people from far off skating on ice after black
pucks slapping
      & skulking each other
              brazen-chested distant-eyed
spitting
      [ ]

so strange this life as syntagm
          in the Book of Faces
stranger this life as logo   franchise graphics
         for disenfranchised demos
who thrive on flesh of the moribund
       who love you when you're dust

                        who weep for you
when you're purchased & kissed
      on the badge
         who grow reminiscent
of the blank sauks who
         when they glimpse gutterpunks
      recall chingachgook
knowing that
      hair stiffens ever-
         fountaining when
    you're moulding
& the bones starch over
     & the eye sockets
        smoothen into snakeskin ::

dwell on "the other slavery"
red scalps
      bloodmalarial eyes
smallpoxed faces
     rede tupi
de televisao

             "and now they have you down
                   as white"

        [.]

            & now in powdered ground
       unspoken for in liquored land contracts
               they have you down
     as redskin   acquiescent
           on breastplate badges
             the sinews
              of you
   [blackhawk]

          moulded over

SALOMA (for R.H.)

(0)

ageless parasite in yr tongue
ancillary to the red ants
freight or comet which interstate
panama papers in bypass
i think of Roberto singing
i think of forms unwrought
i think of disasters in the skull
or mischief veiny & tumescent
en panamá hablamos colibrí
worlds worlding in castor bridge
Cecilia connecting us in cords
intrauterine wolf the dogs nearby
in santiago papasquiaro "sun
veraguas moon is crimson /
what is perpetual in this static
staticians bound by blood
stridentists in xalapa roque
charlemagne frees palestine

on yr tongue sepulchral plebiscite
black ants in future anterior
this serpentine one this doom in yr skin
world systems in disarray
as the world closes in on itself
in the urn ill-made in whiteness
or the industrial excavations of song
as the whipcord contaminant of organ
such as, inasmuch, the humming hues
bridge to worlds, in phantom cities
the cobalt thread of distaffian freedoms
calling the world to recall the gaian
is red / *mexica atahui* / in santiago
mexica perdida" the digital advent
excursions of the state as work of art
fascicles for anthropocentric blues
dalton scanning the radio for zeppelins
in uzbekistan the cherry trees smolder

(1)

    transition from circadian
if we speak of bodies we speak
    we speak of cataclysms we
or detachable, as margins
    the bodies that uncontained
or the crux reminiscent of
    deuteronomies filter the sail
on a hillside i meet you &
    the wholeness that once was
on a hillside i greet you &
    mumble & men can be wolves
of formation, who fornicate
    we journey for decrepitude
other, sprinkled in atoms
    the aroma reaches us, it is
our hair, to sink into cenotes
    we become our howl we
of the world in panama's
    consent, in praise of the

    rhythm to geodisc, its angles eaten away
of involute languages rusting in oxide
    speak of parasitic flows attachable
at the fulcrum of sleep deprivations
    you, a hand outstretched w/o stone
putrefaction, torment of interpreters
    wind cannot stretch or placate
interlocked fingers draw piscis vesica
    the wholeness that departs you
sparrows flutter in our mouths & dogs
    with each other, packs unrepentant
with mildew and disentangle the mold
    the decay we are when we love each
across pathways strewn with acacias
    clockwork beckoning the other to trim
become immortalized in the sun's stupor
    become our unison on the bridge
ageless strip, in praise of the leopard's
    seaturtle's qubit, in praise of culebra

ALLÁ
for Gary Garay

I.

más allá or what's beyond the Beyond
we flip bricks we stack gringo utopias
in rubikube patterns raisined *paisa*
beneath purpled suns choke on dustdevils
(the 4x4 grid favored by patrons)
you win at *lotería*: alacrán
+ calavera minus hand minus
pinto bean (*el catrín* a distant dream)
& mephisto's trump of coronaries
in calloused marathons *con la migra*
burnt soles desiccant throats   cuauhtémoc's skull
whispering:

> *sal si puedes*
> *aquí hay puro cónfort compa*

look you at what the *Otro Lado* gives us:
60 inch flat screens freeways   furniture
wrapped in plastic   public education
free englishing   mcdonald's everyday
batman piyamas   SUVs like homes
away from home   VHS action films
starring JCVD   Miller "high life"
indoor malls where milk carton flowers grow
in seismic faultlines   star-foto memories
of Perla's greeneyes   & Lourdes when her
perm was blown out   in soft-focus whiteout
the spraypainted starry sky forecasting

> *hijos* & fiscal obligations

fíjate carnal we live to construct
other people's homes so we could mortgage
our own *paraíso* with garage &
Ford included; on wknds *bailamos*
norteño soul in the north of our north
comemos the maize of life in East Los
chambeamos in the back kitchens front yards
in civic parks on roofs in factories
white bldgs craned on the hollywood hills
(But if you lose in *lotería*, if
el diablo loses interest, if you don't
buy into EE.UU. dream-logic then

              you're Apache shredded by two arrows
              then you're saint-death's head
                      crowned in acacias
              then you're Ulysses
              adrift, Inland
                    within Empire's high desert
            Rome   the heat of Hesperides at yr back

II.

forget cards or pentagrammic gambles
we've got hands when manos aren't dealt
we frame labyrinths on wknds w/ what
kapital & desert-think leaves behind:

> basura plastic bottles ladrillo metal wire
> cortes' discarded signage shopping carts
> shortbus bugs bunny   cuauhtémoc's feet
> the heterogeneous lustre of scrap metal
> engine parts shards fractions dot-matrices
> speech-machine that binds us in difference

((oigo mi mamá decir
ánimo mijo échale ganas
y con ganas
> *junto las dalias((*

a mask that smiles now cries later
beaded in huichol craft & xolo tech
brings what we know of allá

aquí
      ((they say
      the toltecs timetraveled
      in statuary((

allá
aquí
              they say
              between Joshua Tree
              & the deep blue sea
              Canaan can still
              be seen

where lotus eaters
morphed into serpent feeders
toltechnology pursuant
of TZCTLIIIPCAAA
))our magick red-blackened in the undertow of re-
   conquista   alert to the Open
               bend of
                     the bow

       ((the obsidian's sapience
            on them bestow:

abalone incantation   ((what the seashell
:: an eclipse in reverse   ((remembers ::
worlds & worlds to come))oceanic smelt
in this one   ))even
in aztlán   ))the desert daze

III.

sal si puedes
aquí hay puro cónfort compa

más allá de este mundo
no hay otro

only this
rotund
glutted
partitioned
gutted
prefab
compartmentalized
bifurcated
racialized
one
        [this one]
grown oldie
but goodie

[on the radio we hear voices

::

on the radio we are dead]

Coda: Tianguis "El Nuevo Paraíso"

entra entra
aquí hay de todo
la miseria de los ricos el placer de los pobres
ponches vampiros molcajetes biónicos licuadoras
aguacates blusas tenedores palillos jugos salchichas
takis paraguas ladrillos santitos máscaras ladrones sangre
de víbora cirios bloques botas de piel de caguama chamarras
de seda chaqueta en privado pantalones de cuero chacales en-
cuerados mujeres vestidas monstruos ajedrez laberintos carnavales
ritos de cuaresma pecadores arrodillados carmelitas bailando cumbias
vírgenes en suspenso películas de terror chanclas rotas cartas de lotería
modelos negras modelos blancas incienso de madrugada cortinas gloriosas
labios cosidos cerdos tortillas hechas de mano carne de res cucharas doradas
pozole tacos de tripa orejas cocidas toldos besados oraciones perdidas mofles [x3]
vestidos de quinceañera pelucas de pelo de león chonies amarillos muñecas ensi-
mismadas cobijas de tela platos de plástico el santo cáliz ensuciado perico coca-cola
motita tinieblas revistas esqueletos televisiones bibliotecas luciérnagas luces lombrices
leyendas :: el paraíso entero
compañero el paraíso de los yanquis el paraíso del neoliberalismo el reino de este mundo
obrero :: carpintero braccro forastero caballero tiroteo mareo tiroteo mareo tiroteo mareo

güero güero entra güero   güera güera entra güera
güero güero güeraaaaa   güero güero güeraaaaa

a sus órdenes güero
a sus órdenes güera

THE LOVE SONG
OF HERMAN POOLE BLOUNT

because i believe   in revolutionary
love   the onyx   of my beloved's   eye
is found   in the gazelle's

throaty leap

from dooms

of skin & in

the octave's

duplicity ::

because i believe   in revolutionary
love   the place   i know of
in alabaman kitchens   or at employ-
ment agencies   in chitown's   infirmaries
disciplines me   & meets me   half-
way be-   tween death   & sun's

gaze ::

because i believe   in revolutionary
love

because i believe   in revolutionary
love

because

i believe

****

****

hued man   hewed man

human
is the beast that perishes
dwell on flesh   make it glow
human
is the color that fades
dwell on blackness   make it grow
human
is the planet that folds
dwell on gravity   make it flow

    Baldwin says
behind the white race is one who is nameless

    Ra says
something wrong between whiteness & the sun

    (in) what consists this ( )visibility
in new york   in chicago   in birmingham
    what is it
to stand inside visibility outside it

what is
visibility

****

****

why are certain ensembles
more visible than others
is there a law for it   is there a physics
or a multiverse for it

between life-giving & life-taking
do the stars
delay such discrimination

****

****

hued man   hewed man

Ra says
i'm not mortal
    anyway

               parallel to amorous
                 conjuncture

somewhere snug
in pluralisms
of a distinctive nature

        a grotesque postdiluvian planet
        rotates
           rolls on

    you in it
        this lonesome
  atavism

    you on it
      this ark pulled

   by "ropes
     of wind"

****

****

      his true penelope was
always epistrophee //
      but speculate, you, on keys in porcelain //
if we start *eau forte* w/ a supersonicks, of jazz ::
      we'll land on Afro-Atlantis, place of proto-
Dravidian speech-
      acts // where futures simulate
ancestral pastnesses // & rethink our inner blackness ((thee 1st
      human, in her blackness // in Edakkal trans-
versals stretch sound, in cape gear // sunology restores
      edicts of the kingdom of NOD //
what Mackey informed the medics
      when green cellular bodies r(i)ot in shafts
of sun by waters of Indus // remember: EL is the sound
      of JOY // EL is springtime
in Chicago // of a time when RA crossed over
      al otro lado & made of love
a monument to erotion //

****

****

// of flight & the infolding,
            of the inside of the inside of non-
visibility // he sez :: when you're arche-
            typal :: braindaemons adorned in chrome((
hearken you to Realville's discotheque in the year 3000((
possess yrself! // the sunsong that sutures
            yr shipwreck reanimates you to silhouettes
of island // a velvet saturn horoscoping
            the emergence of *tristes tropiques*
in bassism as realism :: rhythm quarries
            us in the bass-ism of chinagate // an asteroid's
tapestry gawdspells the lunacies of apocalyptic Trumpets
            // at dusk cool jetstreams enshrine
the black suns' cornucopias // we still here   *we gonna be*
            Sun   when sun comes out we gonna
                    be ready
                            be ready
                    be ready

                    you won't see his face((

                em-
        phatic &
                        pris-
            tine a-
mong

        the stars

****

linger, at stardust
a rainbowed bee-eater's bathing
repellent of death's rapturous
heckling   surgical machines
                to captivate
such
profuse sub-
limation
                sub-
        rosa cruciate, in no sense
                terminal

as stately, a blue heron's essential neck
sentencing the fish sequences :: reading
migrations in meaning & copious with
silver in their mouths

        the speckled & glassy
        Isis piecing
        her
        pronounced
                meshes

extinction they say motivates vernaculars, aeration
    like the rooting of
        bipeds in speech acts
                ((uni-
    vocal the remonstrances
  situate our vitals
this is gathering   this is the gathering
    gather you, round us
      you gather us   ((the We
  in volte-face the trans-
-versal, unto a metric of contagious witnessing
    we require, that our patrons
      know whence we
      emerge   ((indefinable,
            like water at the rim
              blurry, overt

    in the shade
deer sez dis is da summit of kulchurs
    grass inside, sea unsurrendering
      shaman sez i see Isis
      crafting Ojibwe from afterimage
  green resin from the 3 fires
           ((*raza* lives on in the organs
           they vehicle &
           sing out of

our language stretches across lunar
        loneliness, reflections in the glasspool
                tilt menomonee
                twd interface & origin
        craft of some peculiarity
indefinable as the graze
of mosquito on elkhair ((in october prism)
        or rice fields wild in contiguous wind
                the *turnvaters* of the german athens
        still unreckoning of
                minute curse or scar tissue
what health disregards
        in algae's blooming fire
the slow death of mitochondria
        encased in lung ::
                but you gather our continuity
        in blood's maplewood
                        these songsters
        caught up in their own voicings
                ((a few miles

                                out a few
                        kilos in
the multiple We we
        are, browned by concords
                we hardly form-
-ulate, the districts
        innumerable & emblazoned
                in omni-
waking

theta is the first dream   in the ear
of night   theta travels on the 808
((the metabolic break

              the rift in yr heart)
& resounds in the emptied lovesongs
of the redstart's refrain   the world
annihilates its spectrums & submerges
what intelligence we have of color &
communal form   theta is the 8th
letter in our entropic   theta is
the 1st letter in thanatos   & yet
we resist   the daedal unbecoming
we resist   the lettering of our skins
in birmingham   public excess
shall be required   in chicago
public excess   shall be required
class vectors do not mark our bodies
an invisible union besets us in Set's
theory ((the project of enumerating
our schemata at the margins of race
)) no, we are sunken as stone lizards
in Ra's gaze   the sun dazes our
politic in a mire of twittery dialect
((what is mimetic caption in slow
     violence   of glacial melt
     at day-
     break's   cataclysm?))

the mages of "harmonic systems"
trump our urgency   wash out our
difference in the mainstream bath-
water   normalize what has always
been a fracture in the surface level
of engagement   & yet we resist
the equations of sameness we surge
on the 808   we seek 8 diagrams
for the 5th assessment we call out
the entities of marginalia   voices
unsurrendering of census bureaus
unseen voices in the desert   white
bears   in striations of apocalypse
flood them with yr faces   flood
them with the wake   of yr velocity
flood them in homan square where
the Black Cube glistens   deform it
untrammel its aesthetics of silence
make no butchery of yr conscience
send out waves of you

                         send out waves
of peregrine voices

                         at the porcine

Tower, heralded

                         only by nightfalcons
who signal yr

                         ascension yr centri-
fugue

HOMMAGE À JEAN BAPTISTE POINT DU SABLE

```
****
*****
******
*******
********
*********
**********
```

And I say that between colonization and civilization there is an infinite distance; that out of all the colonial expeditions that have been undertaken, out of all the colonial statutes that have been drawn up, out of all the memoranda that have been dispatched by all the ministries, there could not come a single human value.

AIMÉ CÉSAIRE, DISCOURSE ON COLONIALISM

How blue can you get? Black. So your mind needs to go all wintry to see the nothing that is there through the nothing that is not. Understand this as a play of presences, not absences— or of presences held within a general absence that is, in fact, not there. It's winter but it's Sunday and the fire's already been lit. The nothing that is not there appears, but only from its own perspective, to surround the nothing that is.

FRED MOTEN, BLACK AND BLUR (CONSENT NOT TO BE A SINGLE BEING)

```
**********
*********
********
*******
******
*****
****
```

vacancy of tomb   by the lakeshore the fusion & cry
of redcheeked cardinals   the riverspeak which speaks

of correlation
at end of daybreak   in the forcefield of
pecuniary corrections: fur trade tales of black fox   gunflints

& flintlocks
awls & glass beads exchanged for marten & otter skin
kettles & axes for beaver & bearheart on bark canoes   width & scale of

diffuse flows
a throng assembling in dire cold the instinct to monopolize
what can't be caged or enframed what resists equation   emergence of

capital fervor
contra wilderness   the machines of civilizing schemery
that make shanties out of groves   that enslave the thought

in time-filled men
what makes objects of people & spreads its cancer
across contiguous ecologies   the sundering of organs &

the scalping of skins
at some instance of advent a father of nationtime
blackbelt migrations in his eyes   the occulted patriarch strikes

fire in the freeze
))fire in his eyes   lumen in his face))   as he worlds within
his solitude the increments of decision: lake cabin in the wood

bordered
in the black sand at nightbreak the deerskins flapping
in carved wind   the Métis speech of hybrid forms out of sync

with whiteness

the remains of a man piecemealed by tradition's
antique cognomens   who belongs to no one but his own flayed
                                                    iridescence
who smokes in the evening the day's accoutrements
who is part indigene part afrofuturist part creole part francophone
                                                    dereliction
jailed in Mackinac he rehearsed his knowledge of white men's
doublings & played sandman to their dream syndicate ((*je suis*
                                        nègre dégagé))
speaking two tongues he spoke a third: commerce of fugues
he knew the tribal routes   he cut open the buffalo heart & showed
                                        them their iniquity
at the Pinery the tribes delegated for him ((give us
a man we see ourselves in)) & the whites were persuaded to give
                                        him his title
Sieur du Sable   of Nouvelle France ((on one side))
freed haitian son of slaves ((on the other)) & yet black on
                                        both sides
the all black core of a historically black metropole
compounded in him as the crimson rings of saturn in the redwood's
                                        vertigo
he self-generated in time as dustmotes generate in a shaft
of sunlight   at the margins of language or memory   decolonizing
                                        vision's prejudices
for what is divested in pigment or countenance
his sightless figure prepossessing the gross figurations of blank
                                        generational privilege
in a catalog of his personal effects pictures of Lady
Corollary   or allegories of black shamans   "Love and Desire
                                        or: *the Struggle*"
& the magick he practiced kholed as the remembrance
of invisibilitas in the fallen blankfaced world ((& such ability as
                                        disappearing at will))

statues preceded him   portraits fabricated his visage
presidents reinvented his figurality amongst the ruins of colonial
                                                            patterns
dreams of Toussaint at nationtime   a hope resplendent
in the reduction of binaries to the eloquence of blackblood in brown
                                                            skin
a spectral promise of mestizaje lurking at the margins
a city defined by its blackness   founded by blackness   the alpha &
                                                            omega
of rhythmic congregations   ((Jean-Baptiste + Kitihawa
unisoned in Cahokia   creole + potawatomi dalliance))   a catholicity
                                                    demonstrative
of future racializations in the future that never became future
        a past that unswerved the past   a moulded grammar unmoored in
mirrors
        unearthed from sand's memorandum   the face's queer involutions
        evolve registers of emeralded organisms   black heralds at crossroads
        conditioning an approach of convolute formations by some distance
mazed
        in the evil flowering at lakeedge   sun's cutthroat dialect   lisping *s'il vous plait*
        to the astral lineages   (((bring us a future we deserve bring us
an ark
        to harmonize the chords   to fracture sameness's intentional inflections
                bring us towards belonging   in a past unswerved   a futurity
consonant
                with the visionary company of trade & barters at variance
                with the contagions of filigreed acquisition   (((is culture praxis   when it
                abstracts the human topos   discords the geomantic inertias

uproots
      what we know of root & branch ((& kestrel))   recurrence absconded
    from river noumenon   36 glass tiles of heat-death   our singing soaked in chromatics
      love's aegis beneath 36 opacities   blacknesses blooming is us like
blue flowers
      at break of dawn   bring us mort rather than gauge   bring us
   an Ark to bind the cosmic race   what grows in the cracks of color
      what fulfills our longing for sameness   the anthro in the spectral-
-photometry
      a poetry of portraits of pictures of decapitated men   the unseen
  as the scenography of contractions   black sand in the crevices
      molecular as bone is under microscope   a trail of tears in fabric
saturated
      in snot & stippling   the corrosive kleptocracy of fresh liberalisms
malaise marshmellowing in green wounds   the corpse's occult
      knowledge cradled in a shaman's wand   our lettered savage
tongue
      Du Sable's vacant eyes   the prefigural speech which made monarchs
of mulattos   ministers of mestizos   brasilwood burning red as
      a self-eating star   the cold that curates the intellect of freezing men
raciality
      a distant memory   Santo Domingo a more distant dream
Saint-Marc a dream of desuetude   Saint Charles a dream of disinterment
      the sleep as deep as bone under kaleidoscope

                              diamantine
              face

      spread as fissures of fire in the cracking coal   who are you
   in the contaminant technocracies that profile and police   who are you
           beneath Linnaean taxonomies & black sands   whose neck
   under pale hands distraught holds a coiled song beneath   whose hands
           implicate the black glove & revolutions of incarcerated
   panthers pacing the steel bars   whose eyes delimit our formlessness
           in the baptismal michigan ˙ coolness of blue horizons
   on the archetype of slain backs   who are you in the dusk wanting
           the whale to swallow you   who are you corralled in
   gothic south scripting epistles   who are you at the limits of reason
           productive of invisible bestiaries   who are you on 75th
   & Pulaski murmuring in drum talk   who are you in the empty edifices
           of Altgeld Gardens   in Cabrini-Green   in Robert Taylor
   who are you on the streets of Bronzeville breaking glass & hymns
           "in the exceeding sun"   who are you in studs &   "bareheaded
   shoveling   wrecking   planning   bldg   rebldg"   at crease
                                                        at fulcrum

          …in the black sands))

                              ((at daybreak…

****

CODA: LOVE CALL

that love has its own paralysis
when we face the wall
beyond charmed sleep   (i remember
in the valley of coyotes once, the anxiety
of waiting for a tide to break   (in a cafe
            where they served cortados

                                    the size of lattes

when i wore the mask
you called my true face   (& still am
            in some rupture

                                    (in love or out

to which world are we called?
            this silverglobe this
            one you are in   (with you &

                                                again

missing the color coral
            when i glimpse salmon
wading in those rivers deepend by yr coppery
sunkist eyes

                        (to see things, for
                        example,

                                    as you see them

recalling what we were
before we were

                    irrecoverable, this feeling of felt
on my tongue   lacking yr crystalline lexeme
        to respond to, to
                            lavish attention upon &
                    simulate unconsciously as we fold lastnite's
        dreamt-in blankets
soft port-of-call treble
            as calming as the shedding of twilit skin
                    caressed by lovespasms
yr voice like daylight sliding
on windowpanes, as afternoon darkened
into night-thoughts
                    lying awake
remembering former
selves   better
        selves, versions of
who we were
in september cataclysms faraway from saturn's
        stuttering indiscoverable

                                    sirensong

        ((recalling what we were
        before we were

under
cupidity's
cruel sun
i discovered

                        caritas,
                        you

                    ****

106

In 1972, Sun Ra and his Arkestra recorded two monumental albums, *Space Is the Place* and *Discipline 27-II*, at Streeterville Studios in Chicago. The composition and title of this book are, in part, predicated on the significance and immensity of those recordings, which provided a vantage point into the conflicting histories and counternarratives that render Chicago (and other North American cities of its scale) a palimpsest. *Place-Discipline* results from a hyphenated form of vision that holds its differences, in place and in space, together.

"*Terra em transe*" refers to the 1967 film by Brazilian director Glauber Rocha, who was a key figure of the Cinema Novo movement.

"The L of Songlines" refers to the Chicago "L" (elevated) rapid transit system, as well as to the "songlines" (or invisible pathways) marked by and accessed through song, story, painting, and dance in Indigenous Australian animist practice.

"Megapolisomancy" is a neologism first coined by Fritz Leiber in the 1977 horror-fantasy novel, *Our Lady of Darkness*.

The phrase "미래가 없다" (p. 24) in Korean Hangul translates to "no future."

The phrase "neither sun nor death" (p. 32) derives from a maxim by François de La Rochefoucauld: "*Le soleil ni la mort ne se peuvent regarder fixement.*" It also serves as the title to a 2011 book by the German cultural theorist Peter Sloterdijk.

"Steele Glas" (parts ii-iv) obliquely refers to George Gascoigne's long satirical poem of the same title, written in 1576. The meaning here is changed to something distinctly modern.

The phrase "climate of hunter" (p. 51) is taken from the title of a 1984 album by Scott Walker. "Antiphonal / carillons" (p. 52) is taken from a line in Hart Crane's poem "The Broken Tower," and "the autumnal, the wounded" is a loose paraphrase of the opening line of Samuel Delany's 1974 novel *Dhalgren*.

The structure and concept of "Exiles" were suggested by some formal components from Julio Cortázar's 1963 novel *Rayuela*.

"Indian Head Test Pattern" is a black and white test pattern introduced by RCA in 1939 and widely used by television studios during the black and white broadcasting era. It featured a picture of a generic American Indian chief's head adorning a grid of lines and shapes that were used to help adjust the resolution, height, and frequency of the television signal. "Essanay Studios" (p. 71) was a movie studio founded in 1907 and based in Chicago. During its heyday, Essanay released several Charlie Chaplin comedies, and its logo also featured the head of an American Indian chief. "And now they have you down / as white" (p. 76) is a paraphrase of a line from Jimmy Santiago Baca's *Martín and Meditations on the South Valley*.

"Saloma" is a poem that pays homage to the work of Roberto Harrison, who introduced me to the Panamanian *saloma* form, a campesino art of guttural call and response musics.

"ALLÁ" is a poem inspired by the artwork of Gary Garay, and the poem's title and imagery reference several of Gary's art pieces. "ALLÁ" translates from Spanish to "over there," and in Gary's work it expresses what lies beyond the border of vision and desire.

"Tianguis" is derived from a Nahuatl word (tianquiztli) meaning "market." In Mexican parlance, a tianguis refers to a street market or swap meet. "Güero güero güeraaaaa!" (p. 87) is a chant sung by hawkers to lure in customers to a famous ice cream parlor in the city of Veracruz, Mexico. Güero is Mexican slang for "blondie" or "white person."

"Ropes of wind" (p. 91) alludes to the title of a story by Henry Dumas. Dumas was cruelly and unjustly killed for "mistaken identity" by a white transit police officer in a Harlem subway station in 1968. Dumas recorded an illuminating conversation with Sun Ra in 1966, posthumously released in 2001 as *The Ark and the Ankh*.

"Hommage à Jean Baptiste Point du Sable" appeared in an earlier version in *Resist Much / Obey Little: Inaugural Poems to the Resistance* (Spuyten Duyvil/Dispatches Editions, 2017) edited by Michael Boughn, et al. The compositional architecture of the poem is inspired by the sonics and enjambment-style of Nathaniel Mackey's poetry. Several lines and phrases in the poem paraphrase and quote from the work of Aimé Césaire, Carl Sandburg, Gwendolyn Brooks, Studs Terkel, C.L.R. James, and many others too numerous to name here.

I want to give very special thanks to my life partner, Mary Lou Villanueva, who loved and supported me during the final stages of the project, as well as to my parents, Jose and Nellie, and to my brothers and sister, Danny, Steven, and Chelsea.

I also want to extend my warmest gratitude to the friends, colleagues, and mentors who supported me along the way, who had confidence in my work at different stages of my career, and who gave me opportunities to read and perform the poems included in this book. I want to give extra thanks to the advice and support of Edgar Garcia, Rodrigo Toscano, Roberto Harrison, Brenda Cardenas, Gary Garay, Daniel Borzutzky, Rachel Galvin, John Wilkinson, Maud Ellmann, Hannah Brooks-Motl, Patrick Morrissey, Stephanie Anderson, Karen Lepri and Kate McIntyre at Projective Industries, and Sarah Dodson, Joel Craig, Sarah Kramer, Mark Malloy, and everyone at *MAKE* Magazine.

Special gratitude and thanks to Dagmara Genda, for her incredible artwork and friendship through the years.

Above all, I want to thank Myung Mi Kim for having selected this manuscript for publication, and Rusty Morrison, Ken Keegan, Trisha Peck, Gillian Hamel, and Omnidawn Publishing for their enthusiasm, faith, and guidance in bringing this manuscript to publication.

Jose-Luis Moctezuma is a Mexican-American poet, translator, instructor, and editor. His poetry and criticism have been published in *Jacket2*, *Chicago Review*, *Big Bridge*, *MAKE* Magazine, and elsewhere. His chapbook, *Spring Tlaloc Seance*, was published by Projective Industries in 2016. *Place-Discipline* is his first book. Born in San Gabriel, CA, he now lives in Chicago.

Place-Discipline
by Jose-Luis Moctezuma

Cover art:
Dagmara Genda
detail from *Ungrounded Cities ii* (2012-2013)
ink, pencil crayon, acrylic, latex on paper
48x48in, 121.9x121.9cm
Photo courtesy of the artist

Cover and interior set in ITC Serif Gothic Std and Didot LT Std

Cover and interior design by Gillian Olivia Blythe Hamel

Offset printed in the United States
by Thomson-Shore, Dester, Michigan
On 55# Enviro Natural 100% Recycled 100% PCW
Acid Free Archival Quality FSC Certified Paper

Publication of this book was made possible in part by gifts from:
Mary Mackey
Francesca Bell
Katherine & John Gravendyk, in honor of Hillary Gravendyk
The Clorox Company
The New Place Fund

Omnidawn Publishing
Oakland, California
Staff and Volunteers, Fall 2018

Rusty Morrison & Ken Keegan, senior editors & co-publishers
Gillian Olivia Blythe Hamel, senior poetry editor & editor, *OmniVerse*
Trisha Peck, managing editor & program director
Cassandra Smith, poetry editor & book designer
Sharon Zetter, poetry editor, book designer & development officer
Liza Flum, poetry editor
Avren Keating, poetry editor & fiction editor
Anna Morrison, marketing assistant
Juliana Paslay, fiction editor
Gail Aronson, fiction editor
SD Sumner, copyeditor
Emily Alexander, marketing assistant
Terry A. Taplin, marketing assistant
Matthew Bowie, marketing assistant
Mia Raquel, marketing assistant